Lost
Ordinary
Magic

Lost Ordinary Magic

by

Rob Lowe
aka
Supermundane

First published in Great Britain in 2024 by Sphere

1 3 5 7 9 10 8 6 4 2

Copyright © Rob Lowe 2024

The moral right of the author has been asserted.

All rights reserved. No part of this publication may be reproduced,
stored in a retrieval system, or transmitted, in any form or by any means,
without the prior permission in writing of the publisher, nor be otherwise
circulated in any form of binding or cover other than that in which it is
published and without a similar condition including this condition being
imposed on the subsequent purchaser.

A CIP catalogue record for this book is available from the British Library.

Hardback ISBN 978-1-4087-3410-0

Typeset in Wople Pegasus by Monotype

Printed and bound in Great Britain by Clays Ltd, Elcograf S.p.A.

Papers used by Sphere are from well-managed forests and other
responsible sources.

Sphere
An imprint of
Little, Brown Book Group
Carmelite House
50 Victoria Embankment
London
EC4Y 0DZ

An Hachette UK Company

www.hachette.co.uk
www.littlebrown.co.uk

Rob Lowe (also known as Supermundane) is an artist, illustrator and writer from the UK. Born in 1971 in the Midlands of England, for many years he thought that everyone saw the world in the same way he did, until one day, it was revealed to him they didn't. He lives and works in London with ~~three~~ two* plants: the sum total of his responsibility.

---

*One died before publishing this book

Contents

The Alphabet

The alphabet is a code. Without access to the meaning of the code, the shapes are purely abstract.

These letters, in various groups, can be read as words with meaning once we have learnt the code. That these words can then be put together in ways that can have life-changing effects on people is where the magic lies.

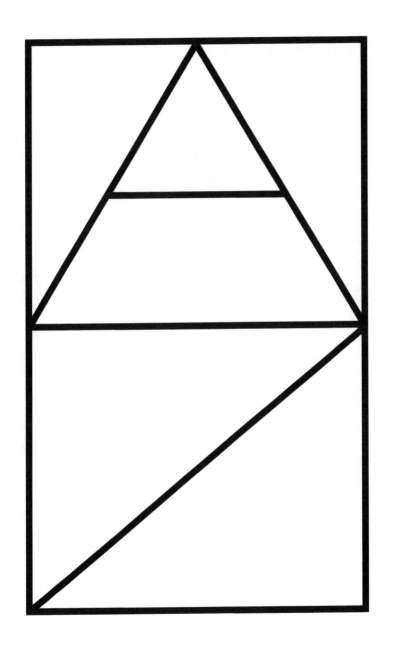

9

Soluble Substances

Some of this book is concerned with things we are expected to accept by the time we reach adulthood. Many of these things still retain a certain magic, even though they have been explained and we have found that explanation satisfactory or we just stop thinking about it and take it for granted. This is a normal way to get through life; to question everything just leads to more uncertainty. The question of why is seemingly infinite.

    That things that are solid can be dissolved in water appears to me to be a kind of magic: something that was once there has now gone. Ta-Dah! But it hasn't. Water with salt dissolved in it will taste salty, with sugar it will taste sweet. The essence remains. There are molecular reasons for this, but let's not go there and just enjoy this everyday disappearing trick.

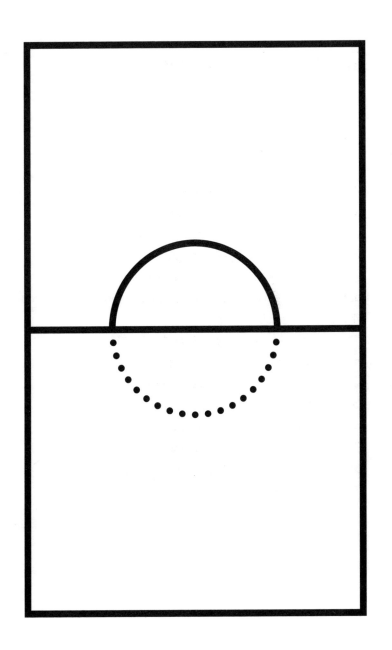

11

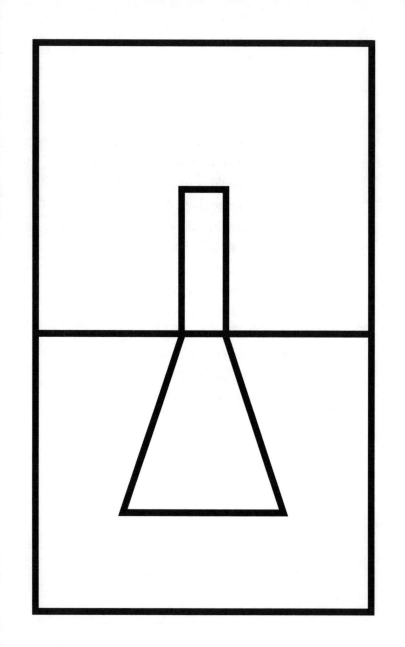

12

Shadows

Once, I saw a video of a friend's child trying to get away from their own shadow. Like a dog chasing its tail, the child couldn't understand that their silhouette belonged to them. No matter how much they ran about, giggling, the shadow followed them, they just couldn't shake it off.

When did I start to accept that my shadow belonged to me? Sometimes I do have a disconnect with it. The extended shadow on a late afternoon beach, for example, stretching my body into something tall and lithe, feels alien to my stocky form. But I am in control of it. If I move, it moves, a graceful avatar projected in front of me. If I wave, it waves back.

Drawing

The ability to capture something on paper is always a surprise to me. I mainly enjoy making non-representational images but I have found pleasure in drawing plants over the past few years. I painted realistic pictures of birds and woodland animals when I was younger, but stopped around the age of 16.

The plant drawings I make are purely about looking. The less I think about what I am drawing, the better they come out. If I think too much, I worry about getting it wrong and often do. So instead I treat the plants as abstract shapes and only draw their outlines.

When I do this I'm often pleased with the end result and it is only after I have finished that I see the lines I have drawn as a recognisable image rather than an abstract one. These drawings are only successful because of looking at what was really in front of me, rather than the preconception of what was in front of me.

Drawing is looking.

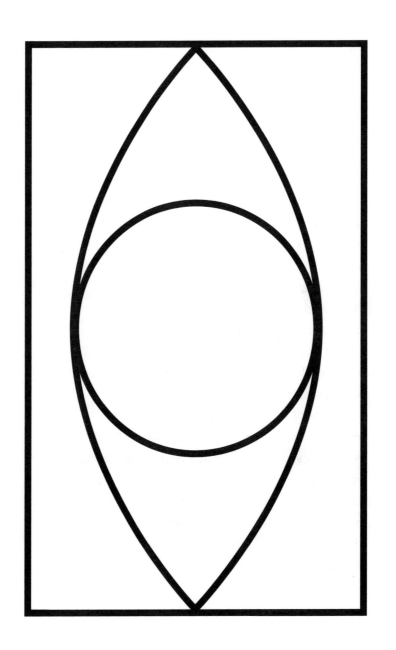

15

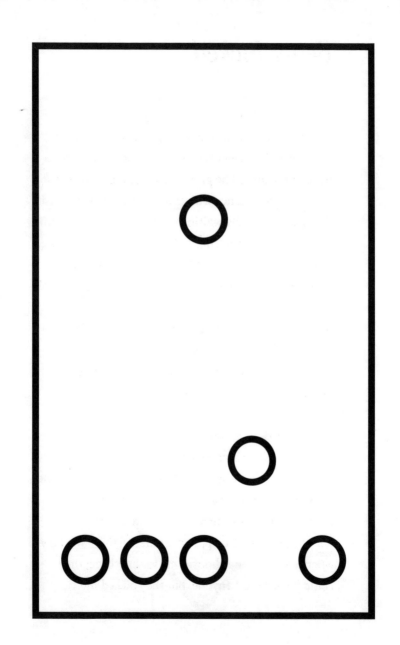

16

Being Picked

At school, we had barn dancing. This took place in the gymnasium where the boys would be lined up in front of the girls. The girls would then pick the boys they wanted to dance with. I would be picked towards the end, awkwardly waiting while the more handsome and taller boys were chosen before me. It was torture. Any school occasion that involved being picked would go a similar way, especially sports. I didn't like school and maybe that came across. In my year, I was the only one into heavy metal music and had mulleted hair to match. The rest of the boys cropped theirs short in the preppy style of the football casuals or experimented with questionable perms.

Because of my experience, I have never taken being picked for granted. When I used to work as a graphic designer and go for interviews, I was always surprised when I was offered the job. Out of everyone who applied they picked me! This isn't some false modesty, but a real surprise that I would be chosen out of everyone who applied. I still feel the same now whenever someone chooses me for anything; they could have picked anyone, but they picked me.

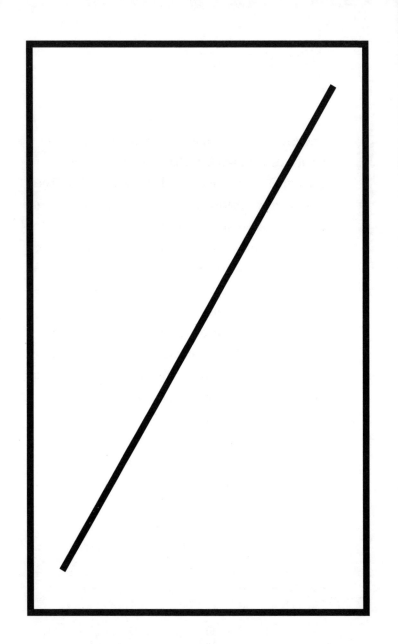

18

Scars

There is a tiny area on my little finger – on my right hand – that you would probably struggle to see; sometimes it takes me a while to locate it. My finger was sliced by a piece of broken glass, whilst splashing a friend in a brook when I was nine years old. As I stood, holding my bleeding finger, the friend ran off and left me on my own.

I'm not very good with blood and struggled to wheel my bike* home, so I threw it into a pile of stinging nettles instead, a sure defence against an opportunistic thief. I can't remember what happened when I got home, or who retrieved it from the nettles, but I had more adventures on that bike so someone must have got it back.

It's a small story remembered because of an even smaller scar.

---

*The bike was a Raleigh Commando, a cousin to the much cooler Chopper, a hand-me-down from my older brother. It was coloured pink, but I used to say it was purple. I'm disappointed in my conventionality.

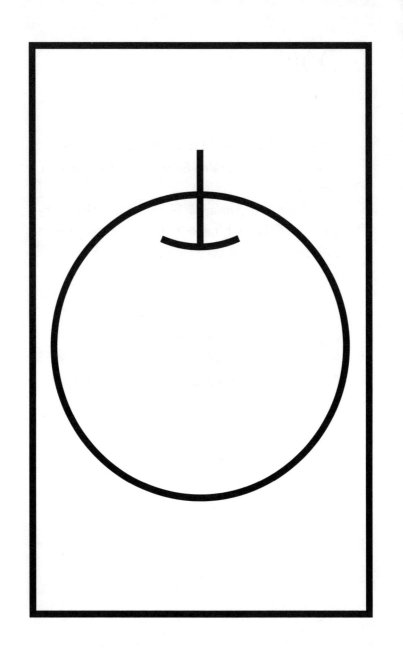

20

Fruit

It has only just occurred to me that fruit exists to be eaten, at least by certain animals, as a means of seed distribution.

While eating an apple I was thinking about why it existed (it has only taken half a century to get to this thought). I realised it had seeds, but why did it taste so good? Why does all fruit (more or less) taste so good?

It evolved to be eaten; a cunning way to distribute seeds. The fruit holds its end of the bargain up by being delicious. We, however, usually flush away the seeds not helping in their dispersal.

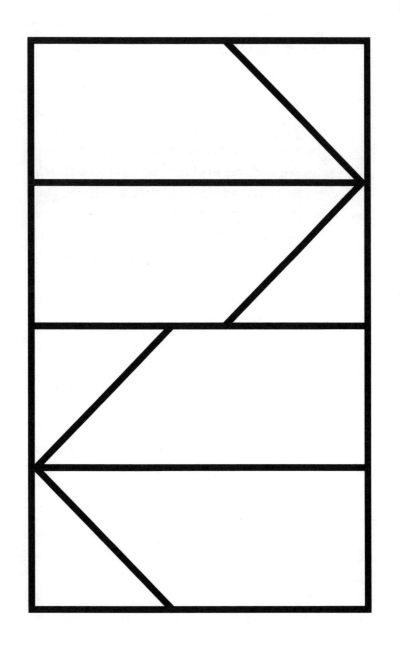

Directions

I have always found directions a little bit mystical. There is something about things being where someone said they would be: 'Look out for a church on your right', and I look and there is a church. On my right! I'm not sure why I have such a thrill when directions are correct and things are where the writer of the directions say they are. I feel under someone else's control and when I reach the place I'm heading to I feel like I have been looked after. Bad directions have the opposite effect of course. I feel betrayed and uncared for. Even if the mistake is mine.

Occasionally, I'm asked for directions when I'm in London. This has more of an effect on me than it should. It always surprises me that someone would think to ask me for directions. Do I look local? Trustworthy? Approachable? If I can give directions it always changes my mood for the better.

24

Electricity

Electricity scares me. It's mainly invisible but being able to hear it, as in the buzzing hum of overhead transmission lines, makes it seem even more powerful. Its place in almost every home is taken for granted and I ignore it as much as possible. I have friends who will unplug everything when they go away on holiday. I don't do this. A few years ago, the studios next to my flat burnt down in an electrical fire started by dodgy fairy lights. I was in my home with a friend when my neighbour knocked on the door and said we should come out, which we did, to a street of firemen and theatrical flames raging from the roof next door. So, I probably should unplug my electrical devices.

Another experience with electricity, which is much more personal, is static electricity. For a while, I wore plastic sandals in my flat, something about them and my floor created static and would give me a shock when I turned on the kitchen tap. It got to the point where I would approach turning the tap on nervously and still jump when I got a jolt. It doesn't happen as much now but every so often I get a shock, in every sense of the word.

Birds (One)

As a child, I was a young ornithologist and
member of the Young Ornithologist Club,
the junior arm of the RSPB (Royal Society for the
Protection of Birds). I'm still a member of the RSPB
and still enjoy watching birds. Usually, if I mention
this, the trigger response is 'are you a twitcher?'
I am not. Twitchers are obsessive. They have more
in common with trainspotters than people who just
enjoy watching birds. It's all about numbers and
rarity for them.

I enjoy the proximity you can find yourself
to birds; some, like the robin, will come very close.
There is also the fact that they can fly (a heron in
flight, for example, is an incredible sight); some make
beautiful nests; some have beautiful songs they sing.
Even the maligned pigeon can be beautiful when
you look past its ubiquity and bad reputation, its oily
neck gifting hidden colours when hit by sunlight in
the right way.

When I was growing up we had house martins
in the eaves of our roof. The Midlands didn't have
the variety of birds the South or the North did –
I had to move to London to see my first jay –

but the house martins returning each year was something I looked forward to. Their black and white swoop and mud-bobbled nests are something I look back on with fondness. By the time I left my family home and moved to London, the house martins hadn't returned for a few years. I don't know why this is or if humans had anything to do with it, but I really did miss them each summer.

For some reason, Tamworth (the town near Fazeley, where I grew up) had a few fairly exotic water birds. There was a stir when we had a black swan appear on the river, an Australian bird that couldn't have flown all the way to the Midlands of England. We also had a mandarin duck, its origins similarly far away, which is still a favourite of mine. The male looks like a painted ornament; I'm always taken aback when I see one in a London park.

Now, I look forward to the first sign of swifts returning; their bat-like flutter and evening screech signalling that summer is on its way.

28

Birds (Two)

I live on a cobbled mews – in a rented live/work studio that my mum calls a garage – which is quieter than it should be, being right next to the South Circular, with its lorries rattling around the corner on their way in and out of London. If I stay on my street I forget what is going on out there, just the occasional siren to break the illusion of calm.

In our little sanctuary we have a few birds that I see most days. There is always a thrill when a goldfinch's song or wren's vociferous trill fills the air. Even the pigeons, that seem to prefer promenading in pairs down the street to flying, are a welcome sight. Most recently, we have had a grey wagtail nesting, its bobbing tail an uncommon sight among the converted industrial buildings. These birds are a reminder, that under the cobbles is dirt and in the past, the whole area was covered by the Great North Wood. The buildings, concrete and cars that replaced the ancient woods are the oddities here, not the birds.

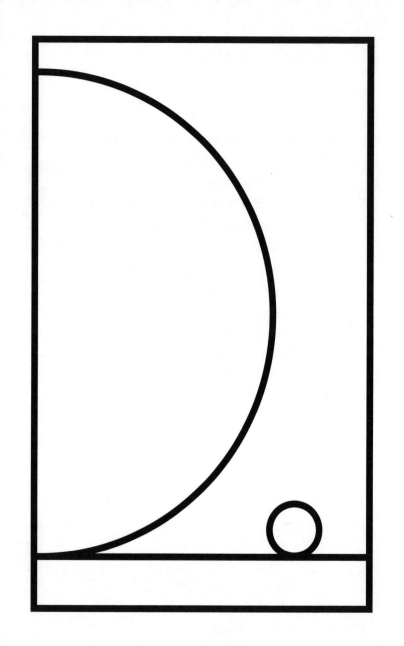

30

Small Things

There always seems to be a love of big things. Small things are also loved but are often seen as cute and lacking gravitas.*

The love of the big things means we can miss taking joy in the details of everything around us. A single teaspoon of soil, for example, contains more living organisms than all the people on Earth.

Of course, big things are only big because of small things (and vice versa). We are the world to the bacteria that live within us. Imagine them finding out there's a whole universe out there!

---

*As a 5ft 4in man, am I a small thing?

Mistakes

As I get older, I have become more and more convinced that new things happen by getting things wrong rather than getting things right. The modern world doesn't deal with getting things wrong very well and as such is risk averse. This stagnates creativity meaning it is easier, and safer, to repeat what has worked before rather than risk failure. The box office sequel being the perfect example of this: they will always make money regardless of how good the film is. So why risk something new when it might fail?

Some bands I'm a fan of say that when they started, they were trying to sound like their heroes but didn't have the skill or knowledge to copy them. Through their inability to mimic their sound, new sounds were made. Getting it wrong created a new right.

33

Spontaneity

The space to be spontaneous, without fear of judgement, is the only space that can birth creativity. Spontaneity is creativity.

Ballpoint Pens

There is something about the iconic Biro that I will always love. They are reliable – allowing for the occasional leak or unforthcoming nib – and give their usefulness in such a humble way. In comparison to the wonderful but needy fountain pen, the Biro can seem throwaway.

I have rarely used up all the ink in a Biro, usually losing the pen before its well is spent. Out of the limited colours: black, blue, green & red,* green has always been my least favourite.

Nowadays, online artists draw photorealistic images using Biros that people coo and woo over: 'You won't believe this is drawn with a Biro!' Such is the lack of expectation in the quiet utilitarian that is the ballpoint pen.

---

*I'm sure you must be able to get other colours now.

Coincidence

Some people believe in fate: *there is a reason for everything* they might say. I do not think that is true. I think that everything can be given meaning, but this doesn't just happen, it requires active interpretation.

Often when I'm writing, someone on the radio (always Radio 4), will say the same word at the moment I am writing it. This is pure coincidence and it would be hard to read anything into it, however, something does happen, a connection for a second that hadn't been there before.

Sometimes when someone calls, it can feel like I was just thinking about them: *I was just thinking of you* I might say. Almost as if I have willed them into existence. My feeling is that we are thinking about everyone we know, and have known, all the time and the brain protects us from the babble so we don't go mad.

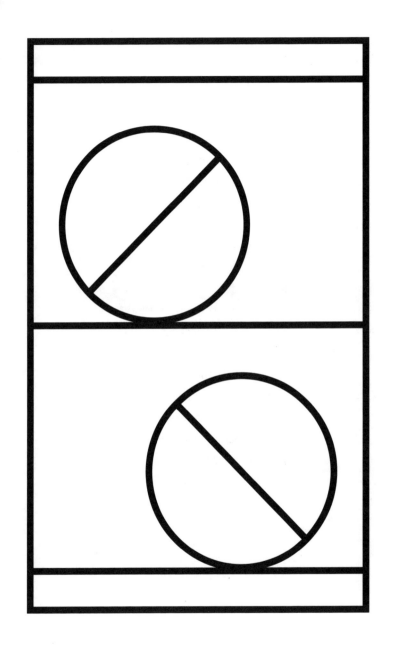

38

Ghosts

Not the supernatural kind – I don't have any sense of those kind of ghosts being real – but objects, words or sounds embedded with memories. These ghosts can be of people living or dead; moments or places.

I have lost or thrown away so much of my past that very little in the way of ghost objects exist. There are smells and tastes, however, that will spark a visit from a ghost of my childhood.

The funny thing is that the things that meant something to me in the past, that I no longer have, I can still picture. The memory (or ghost) of those objects is enough to bring back the memories they in turn contained. Of course, I cannot remember the objects I have forgotten, so I have no idea how many memories I have lost, but that is OK. It is easier to ignore the ghosts of the things you have forgotten.

Here's a poem I wrote a while ago about this kind of thing:

> *She slipped her bare foot into the shoe*
> *Recoiling as it felt the ghost of her grandfather*
> *In the ridges he had left behind*

Books (One)

Cheap, second-hand, paperback books are living
things. From the time they leave the shop, crisp and
identical, each one takes on a different life from all
the other copies of the exact same thing. Dog-eared,
stained and written in; they are a reflection of the
humans that have read them. They can be forms of
social history and finding marginalia or ephemera
hidden away in the browning pages is always exciting.

Books (Two)

There was a time when the physical book looked like an endangered thing. Digital versions felt like the future – whole libraries could be carried around in a dull grey tablet, with a duller grey screen, that told you how far you were through the book in percent. I own one (although I haven't looked at it for a couple of years), it is a practical way of reading books whilst travelling. For a short while I felt it would make me read more; tackling some lengthy books which felt less intimidating than the weighty physical copy.

But I missed the object. I missed putting it on my shelf when I'd finished (or not, with the hopeful idea that I would, one day). My flat is full of books. Just a couple of shelves took all the paperbacks they could and now piles of books have appeared wherever the space allows, like wordy weeds. I find being surrounded by books deeply comforting; the ones read and the ones yet to be read. All those words leafed together; all reminding me of the stories they contain.

Books are friends to those who love them.

Reading Fiction

I've had an argument a couple of times with people about reading fiction. I'm not sure if they are just winding me up but the argument goes that they don't read fiction because *it's just made up* and *it's better to read about facts.* My response is: reading fiction helps me understand people better.

The slowness of reading, which means a book can take a week or more to finish, helps you occupy another world in a way that a film or podcast can not. Films and podcasts are experienced in a relatively passive way, whereas a book requires your input in order to get the most out of it – you create the world it occupies and give flesh to the characters. Each reader will have a slightly different world that they have created.

Women read a lot more fiction than men.* Make of that what you will.

---

*A YouGov poll found: Women are much more likely to prefer fiction (42%) than men (29%).

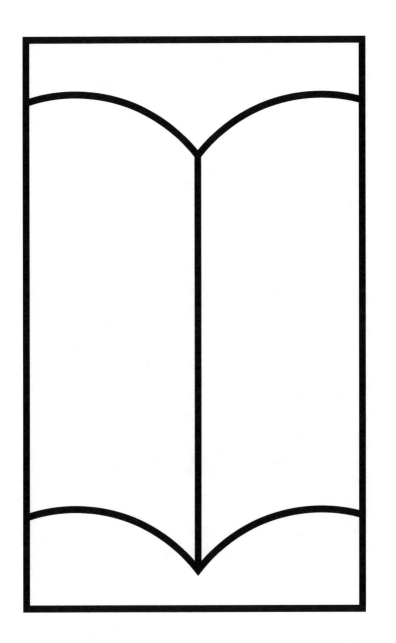

43

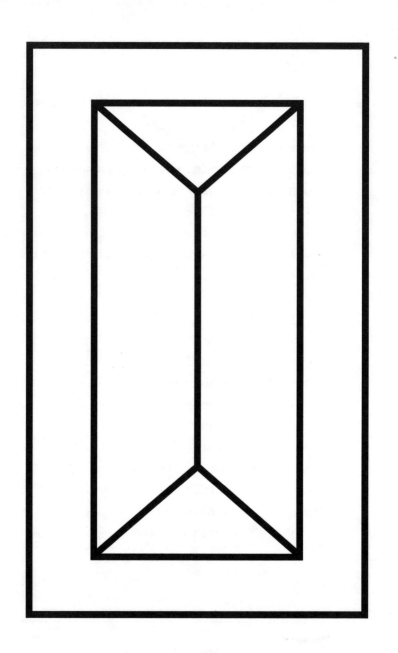

44

Bricks

I have grown up in a world of bricks. Nowadays
many buildings are being built with glass and metal,
things that do not really show their age; new brick
buildings do not feel the same as old ones, I'm
not sure why this is. It could be the design of the
buildings or that the bricks have changed, but I think
that it is that the grime of time hasn't softened and
coloured them.

I had a friend visit from California* and she
was fascinated by the brick buildings everywhere in
London. As we passed Battersea Power Station[†] I felt
just as amazed by this huge building, that is made of
cuboids not much longer than 20cm each, as she was.

My aunt and uncle had a pet brick. I cannot
remember the name of it, I think it was whatever was
written on the brick. It sat near the front door as a
talking point: *what's that brick doing there? It's our pet
brick. It's called* (I can't remember).

Why are bricks so appealing?

---

*See page 82
[†] One of the largest brick buildings in the world. Built with approximately
6 million bricks.

Remembering

I find it hard to remember things.

For some reason, I don't remember much of my childhood and have forgotten quite a lot of my adult life too. I often struggle to recall things – especially names – but when they do pop into my head, it feels like they have been dropped in. Where were they and why couldn't I access them?

Remembering, and using, people's names is something I wish I was better at. When I meet someone good at it, I'm always reminded how much of an important skill it is. When I don't remember someone's name – which usually happens straight away after I have asked them – it sends out a signal that I don't care enough to remember.

I tell myself that I am OK when people don't remember my name, and that is true, but I forget how wonderful it feels to have someone remember and use mine.

The (Analogue) Telephone

Mobile phones are not ergonomically made to have a conversation on for any length of time. Their flat design works much better for texting or video calling than traditional voice-only telephones. Often phone calls drop out or you have a bad line ('can you still hear me!?') and you end up with a red-hot ear. Bluetooth headsets can stop this but who wants to be *that* person.

The telephone of my past was an ergonomic object that you could talk on for hours. With mobile phones there is never the anticipation of who will be on the other end (I never answer unknown numbers). Their name is there, sitting on top of your own reflection looking back at you.

In *Ways of Hearing*, by Damon Krukowski, he talks about how the sound of phones is now different; using compression to remove anything deemed as unnecessary to make the digital file as small as possible. The result is a flattening of the voice and a removal of context. Our voices made more robotic and less nuanced; less human.

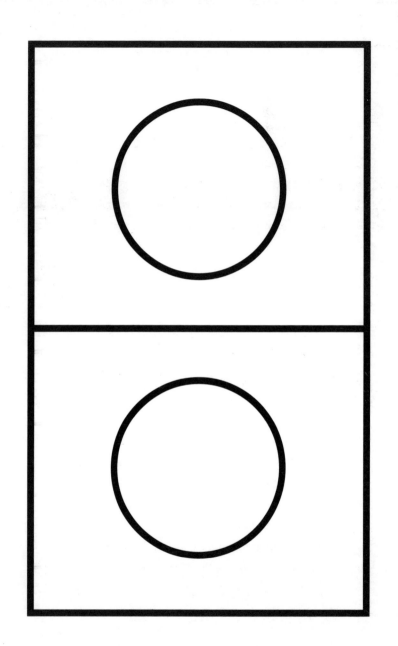

48

Mimicry

I'm not bad at mimicry. Sometimes I can do an accent or an impression, but I have little control over it and it's patchy at best. What I find surprising is that it is possible, without knowing how you are doing it, to make your voice sound like someone else's.

I tend to mimic people naturally without knowing I'm doing it; my accent (a soft Midlands accent) takes on the qualities of the person's voice I'm talking to. I mimic physical gestures to some degree too. I never realised I did this until recently. I wish I didn't know because now I catch myself and moderate it.

Mimicry can also be used to taunt and mock people, this kind of mimicry taps into our insecurities: I don't really sound like that. Do I?

I recently heard the singer Jarvis Cocker talk about seeing someone do an impression of him on the TV program *Stars in Their Eyes*. The contestant mimicked his idiosyncratic dance moves as well as his voice. Jarvis said this made him feel deeply self-conscious of how he moved and made dancing harder and less fun.

Photocopier Paper

The cheap A4 white sheet is an invitation to be creative. It is not a precious thing: a sheet costing little more than half a pence. It is as unthreatening as a blank page can be.

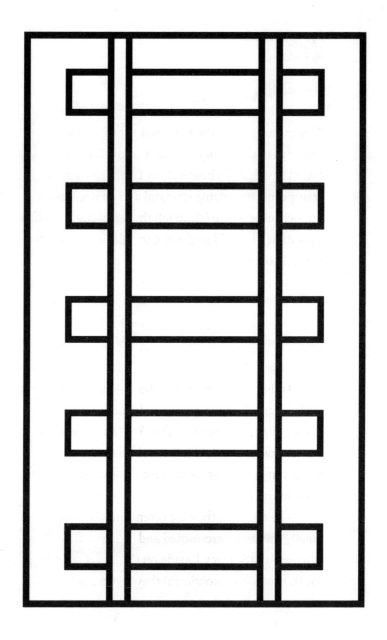

Trains

This is more about the potential of train travel
rather than the reality – at least in the UK. When
train travel is at its best it is my favourite form of
transport. I find flying stressful and an unpleasant
physical experience (although the act of flight itself is
incredible). I would prefer not to fly if it wasn't often
the only option.

I haven't driven for a long time and car journeys
can be freeing: music blasting and going directly from
A to B without struggling with luggage. But often the
journeys are on bland motorways or spent stuck in
traffic jams. Or both.

Trains let you see the countryside change as you
whizz along. You can get up and move around. There
is usually the option of a table. You can have a beer.
You can daydream looking out the window or read or
watch a movie. Most of my best ideas come to me on
train journeys.

The reality is they are often delayed, noisy,
smelly things. Overcrowded and too expensive. This
is a shame; a journey I made on the bullet train in
Japan shows how wonderful they can be.

Thunder

I'm often filled with nerves and adrenaline at the crack of thunder. That nature can make such an awesome sound is a reminder of its power.

Thunder, for me, is forever linked to the film *Poltergeist* (as are my feelings about clowns). I watched it when I was quite young, around the house of the lead singer of a band called Magnum. I guess I was about 14, probably old enough to handle the film, but I hadn't seen many horrors (I still don't like the genre very much), and this one stuck in my head. The child in the film is scared of thunder and is told to count between lightning flashes and thunder claps. If the time between the two gets longer then the storm is moving away. You can guess this doesn't end well.

Now, I'm not as scared of thunder as I was, but it always brings to mind this film, however unwelcome.

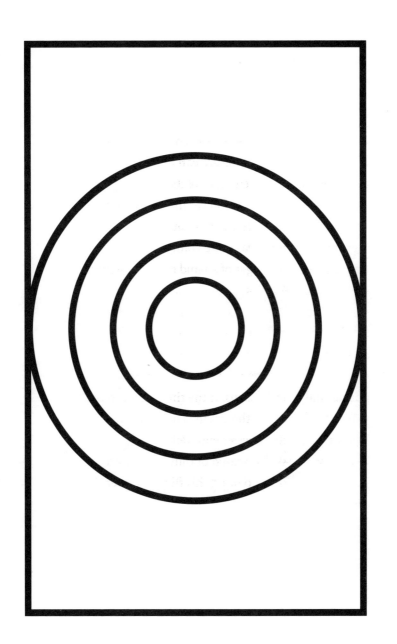

55

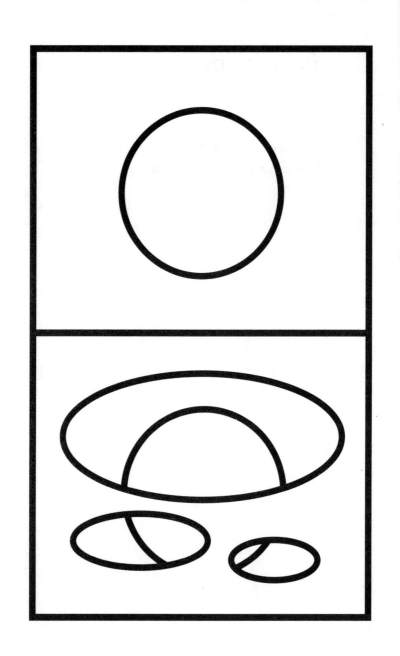

Reflections

I still don't really understand how reflections work.
How can a puddle contain the sky?

Letters

When I left home to go to art college, I had been in a new relationship for the whole of the summer holidays. It was an intense couple of months and then I moved 160 miles away. We kept up a long-distance relationship mainly through letters.

Almost every day a letter would arrive in the North East that would have been posted the day before in the Midlands. They usually came the day after they were posted and the disappointment when there wasn't an envelope, with its recognisable handwriting, was acute. At my parents' house is a bag with hundreds of these letters. I feel guilty to say this but they are mostly quite boring and I will have to get rid of them at some point.

I wish I had the ones I sent, they would have been a record of my years at college. Essentially I was posting my diary. I'm not in contact with my ex-girlfriend so I don't know if she kept my letters. I doubt it. Why would she? But then, why do I have hers?

You can still send a letter with a first class stamp and it will get to most places in the UK the next day (for now at least).

59

Not Thinking

There are times when thinking is very important and necessary and people, generally, should do more of it, but there are times that it gets in the way and stops you from doing or making things.

I have heard quite a few artists, poets and musicians talk about being a conduit or an aerial for ideas coming from somewhere else. I don't think they believe there is some mystical delivery system of creative ideas – where would they come from and why? Rather, that when we stop overthinking, we can access parts of our brain that are not as easy to get to when we are thinking about it. Things we are not even aware of knowing, only showing themselves when we don't try to locate them.

Things Found in Books

On page 40, I briefly mention the enjoyment of finding things in second-hand books. Often they are ephemera (such as tickets, receipts or invites), which give a small insight into the past owner, or owners, life. My favourite things are the few letters I have found. An example of this are two that were stapled inside of a copy of *The Barnyard Epithet and Other Obscenities; Notes on the Chicago Conspiracy Trial,* a book I picked up mainly for the typographic cover, which made an over-long title into a beautiful design.

The letters are short, but potent, accounts of the late '60s – early '70s America and reflect the hopelessness of a time when the hippy optimism of the '60s was crumbling. They are addressed to a man called Reg Budd, who Connie, the writer of the letters, names in full twice in the first sentence, of the first letter – which made me fall in love with her a little bit. The rest of the letters cover, among other things, the trial of the book, the comedian Lenny Bruce, an oil slick and various underground newspapers of the San Francisco Bay Area. These pieces of social history couldn't have been found if they had been emails. They exist because of their physicality and a desire to treasure them.

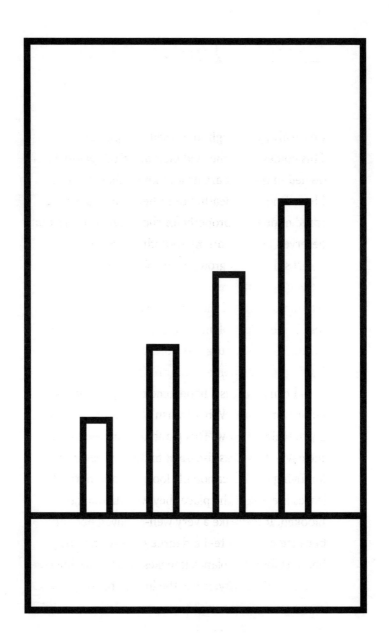

Growing Things

I have always thought of myself as a plant killer.
This comes from the evidence: all of the plants I have
owned in the past are dead. I know that it's not that
I have fingers of death, but rather that I have never
cared enough or properly for these living things that
deserved better than my sporadic watering.

I still haven't grown many plants and I haven't
yielded a crop of veg or even a few herbs. I have one
plant: a calathea. I thought I was going to kill this
too. It is a tricky plant to look after, having been
taken from its natural rainforest humidity and
finding its new home in South East London.

I can't say it is a handsome example of its kind
but it is still alive. What I wasn't expecting was the
joy of seeing it grow. This plant also moves through
the day – the leaves rise up at night. I've never seen
it moving but I occasionally look at it and notice the
leaves are not in the place they were the last time
I looked. It feels like a very well-behaved pet and
because of that I feel a degree of responsibility
I haven't for other plants; it makes its presence known.

It is also fussy: it has the luxury of spring water,
whereas I make do with tap.

The Sun

It hardly needs to be stated that the Sun is an awesome thing; a huge fireball in the sky.

One summer, I was sat under a tree in a park; the top half of my body was shadowed by the tree but my legs were in the sun, I could feel it burning them. I was struck by how hot the sun must be* for me to be physically affected by it from millions of miles away.

For that time, I felt directly linked to the Sun through heat. A cosmic connection.

---

*The surface of the sun is 5505 °C.

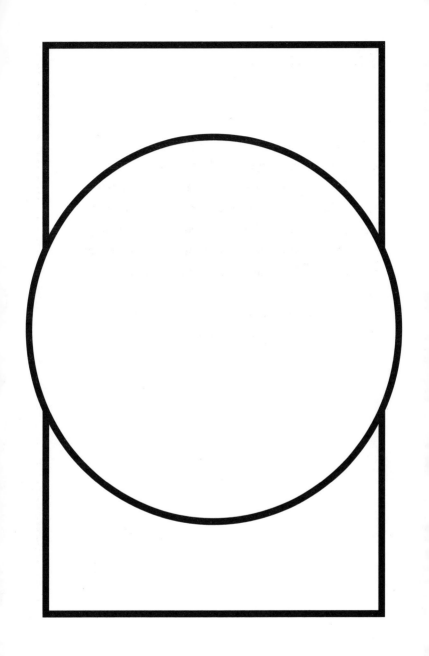

65

Sleep

Sleep is time travel.

Maps

Printed maps are no longer as needed as they once were. The satnav and phone have made them almost obsolete. Unless you are orienteering or in a situation where the analogue, non-battery run, paper map could save your life.

I still like maps. The aesthetic quality as well as their usefulness. One of the only things I have ever stolen was a map from a *Lord of the Rings* book in my school library. Folded and stuck into the inside front cover and printed in black and red, it was too much for me not to have. I feel guilty for this now, especially as I don't know where the map is anymore and haven't for a long time.

I liked using the road atlas on long car journeys. Being the navigator gave me the privilege of knowing where we were in the country and what was coming up. It gave me a sense of place and an understanding of time passing. Now with phones telling you where to go, and often the roads used being anonymous motorways, the journey is something to get done as quickly as possible. No longer taking pleasure in odd town names or knowing when you are near the sea; the shotgun seat now rendered jobless.

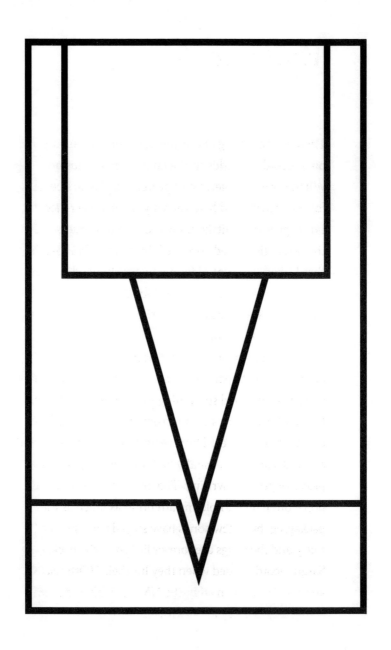

Vinyl Records

There is something about the ceremony of putting
on a record that adds to the enjoyment of music.
When I was younger, I had protective plastic sleeves
for my records and held the vinyl with a reverence
I have given very little in my life. I would obsess over
the often illustrated covers of the heavy metal bands
that I liked. As I got older my tastes changed and so
did the covers. The airbrushed fantasies of the heavy
rock albums were replaced by the 7-inch sleeves of
the indie bands of my teens.

One record label called Sarah became a mild
obsession. Every part of the packaging was used as an
opportunity to add something extra. The record label
had photos of train stations from the Bristol area, on
consecutive releases. The reverse of an insert, that listed
the back catalogue, usually had some prose poetry or
pieces of political writing. The music itself – twee indie
pop – often didn't hold my attention as much as the
packaging, but a few songs have stayed with me until
today and the songs are forever linked to the packaging.
Sarah records closed when they hit their 100th release
announcing it in an ad in the NME (who hated them)
with the title 'a day for destroying things...'

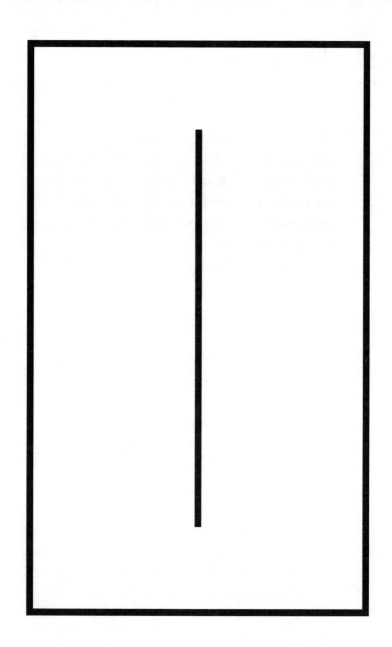

70

Lines

We leave our mark on the world and define our space in it through lines. They are everywhere (physically and metaphorically) and once you notice them they are a clear indication of human activity or control. Even the lines that nature makes only have meaning or beauty to humans.

The line is a deeply human thing that we respond to in many different ways but, fundamentally, on an instinctive level.

Poetry

I never used to understand poetry and mostly concerned myself with the humorous, rhyming kind (which I still have a lot of time for).

I still don't understand a lot of poetry but, at some point, I realised it was OK not to fully understand the meaning of a poem, the words in the order that the poet had chosen affected me and that was enough. I am not that interested in the kind of poetry that has metaphors in every line,* but the kind that either is using clear words in a way that makes you feel *something* or the kind that uses words in a more abstract way like incantations. There is magic in taking something as dead as a word and making it come alive through its careful placement next to others.

---

*Since writing this I have joined an informal poetry group where we talk about poems and poets with a poetry tutor. I have started to take pleasure in all kinds of poetry. Even the ones that feel like cryptic crossword clues.

Bread

Who thought to mill grains and then do all you need to do to make bread? I'm sure there is some evolution that makes sense but it seems such a leap from there being no bread to there being bread.

I love bread. It doesn't love me.

Being in Water

I remember being in Spain, playing in the sea with my girlfriend, picking her up with an ease that came with the help of the water – on land, it would have been an undignified struggle due to my lack of upper body strength at the time. The sea gave me a power that I didn't possess away from it.

I swim in the cold water of Tooting Bec Lido all year round (since the winter of 2017). Something that I never thought I could do now gives me so much happiness. Those freezing cold dips, that have an immediate effect as the water bites the skin and the body goes into a shock coping mechanism, are some of my favourite times. Swimming in the sea or river or lido, it is being in cold water that is important. Being in water is a return.

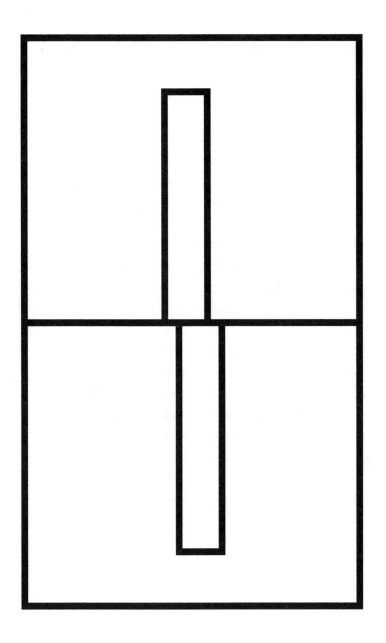

75

76

Clouds

Many people enjoy clouds, many others don't and see them as a scar on an otherwise perfect blue sky, or a forewarning of rain.

I'm in the camp that loves them. Their scale and beauty amazes me. The thrill of being above (or in) the clouds when on an aeroplane is something that has never left me.

As a child, I used to pretend we were a huge spacecraft floating through space by lying on my bunk bed in such a way that I could only see the clouds and sky through the window. On a windy day, when the clouds moved quickly, I could imagine that the clouds were static and it was our house that was moving. I couldn't do it for too long, as it would take a lot of concentration, but, for the minutes when I could convince myself that we were moving and not the clouds, I could actually believe it.

Being Alone

Being alone isn't unusual and is easily achievable,
but there are times in my life when my solitary state
adds to the experience.

Some solitary times:

> Barbera Hepworth's garden on a sunny
> winter's day.
> A room with Van Gogh's *Sunflowers*.
> A room with a Frank Stella painting
> (with no restriction on how close you could
> be to the painting.)
> James Turrell, *Skyspace*, San Francisco.

That these are all art-based says something.
That I have stood in front of a Van Gogh painting
and knew I was the only person, in the world,
looking at it at that moment meant something to
me. I have the same feeling when I'm visiting any
place and I am the only one there. I do not feel
special, I just feel alone, in the best way possible:
out of the billions of people in the world, I'm the
only one doing this right now.

Striking a Match

When I was young, the newsagents in front of our house would sell one match and one cigarette to kids who couldn't afford to buy a whole pack of either: a smoking starter kit. Matches at the time could be struck on any rough surface so the kid who bought the smoking kit had one chance to strike the match and light the cigarette. I never did this but I had a fascination with matchboxes (see page 100). In particular, the stumpy England's Glory and the sulphurous smell of the striking side of the box.

My nan had a jar filled with books and boxes of matches that she collected. They were from all over the world. One book had a cartoon of a naked man on the inside and a match would ping out phallically when you opened the book. She also had one of those striptease pens and would give me weak Cinzano and lemonade when I was 10 years old. It was a different time.

Once, I wanted to make a box of matches (part of a project about household things), called 'A Gift of Fire'. On the box I designed, it had an image of a house on fire and said 'Don't Do This' below the diagram. The gift of fire comes with an amount of responsibility.

Walking

Walking slows down time. An hour walking is different to an hour in a car, an hour watching television or an hour down the pub.

Sometimes when I'm walking I think about how odd it is I can do this act without thinking. That my body can somehow stay upright and my legs move in such a way that I can take myself from place to place. Once I start thinking about it, I feel a bit strange and walking starts to feel unnatural. It doesn't last long and before I know it I'm back walking without thinking about it once again.

Trust

Quite a few years ago I received an email that was
just a poem. The sender had been in touch a while
before about some typefaces I had designed, but
there wasn't much more of an interaction than that.
I can't remember the poem. The computer it was on
has died and I never backed it up. I do know that
I replied with a poem and this back and forth went
on for a few months. This was before social media
so it was hard to find out who it was behind the
emails. I knew it was a woman though and she was
in America.

At some point, we decided to chat – still sending
poems now and again. If we timed it right we could
email each other in real time – usually at night for
me. Then out of the blue she said she would like to
come to London and I said she should.

She did. We hadn't even seen pictures of each
other. We spoke once on the phone as I commissioned
her to make some illustrations for the magazine I was
designing at the time. That was it.

She booked her flight and I said I would meet
her at Victoria (thinking about it now it would have
been better to meet her at the airport). She didn't

know if her phone would work in the UK and back then there wasn't easy access to email. I said to meet at WHSmiths in Victoria if anything went wrong. Something did go wrong, I can't remember exactly what, I remember wondering if I should go home and wait for her to call my landline but, walking across the concourse in Victoria station I saw a girl sitting in front of WHSmiths and I, somehow, knew it was her. We hugged and tried to make sense of what had gone on and the fact that she had waited at WHSmiths until I came.

If this was a rom-com (the story has the feel of a Nora Ephron* film) we would have got together and there would have been a lovely ending where we finally kissed as the camera pans away. We had a wonderful week but nothing romantic happened. She was much taller than me and, as such, felt a bit like a beautiful different species. Still, it was one of the best weeks I have had in London and it happened because she put her trust in me. And I in her.

---

*Nora Ephron is the writer of *When Harry Met Sally*, *Sleepless in Seattle* and *You've Got Mail* (a film that I have watched more than any other).

Telling Stories

Humans make sense of the world through stories for good and bad reasons. When told well, they captivate and build images and worlds; they help us understand each other better.

Without stories what are we?

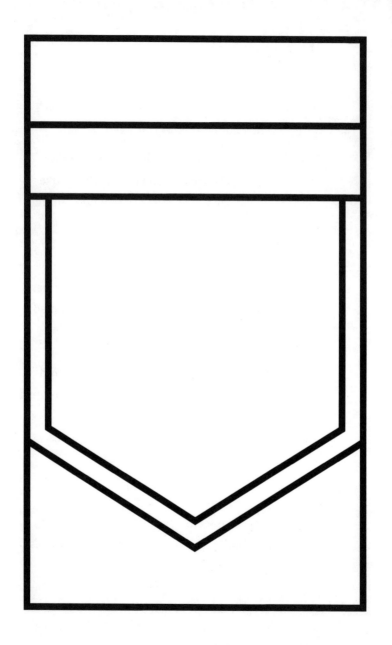

Pockets

I'm a fan of pockets. Especially the type that can hold lots of stuff (at the very least big enough for a paperback book). Having a good size pocket is like always having a bag with you; a place to put a found stone or feather, or an unplanned book purchase.

The sci-fi author Ursula K. Le Guin wrote an essay called *The Carrier Bag Theory of Fiction*.* In it she spoke about an alternative history to the hunter hero, claiming that it would be the things found and made, which were used for gathering (such as '...a gourd a shell a net a bag a sling a sack a bottle a pot...'), that would have been the first cultural devices and affected how we developed, rather than weapons and the bloodthirsty tales linked to them.

We have always needed things to carry things. Pockets are one of those things. They are unheroic, as their precursors were; often used without thinking: stuffed with keys, chocolate bar wrappers or used tissues. Although, if seeing the joy that comes from a dress with pockets is anything to go by, their usefulness is not always taken for granted.

---

*Satisfyingly, the *Carrier Bag Theory of Fiction* is published in a pocket-sized edition by Ignota Books.

Creativity

In Oli Mould's *Against Creativity* (which is much
more against the capitalist use of creativity than
the act itself) he says creativity is the *'power to create
something from nothing'*. This seems to me to place
it in the realms of fantasy and far out of the reach
of normal people or those who do not consider
themselves creative. Nothing comes from nothing
and to say creativity is the act of making something
from nothing risks feeding into the idea of the sole
genius. You can make something that has never
existed before but it would have not have come from
nothing, rather from all the influences, known and
unknown, from your time living in the world.

Creativity, to me, is the act of making –
physically and intellectually. It often includes:
making mistakes, trial and error, and multiple
influences. It means thinking about alternative
ways of doing things rather than the accepted way.
Anyone can do this and it can be taught. It doesn't
mean you will create anything that is good, but then
who said creativity was about making good things
rather than just creating?

Context

Context can take the same thing and make it mean many things, including the opposite.

We live in a world that seems to take things more and more literally and from a single, personal, point of view. Descartes said 'I think, therefore I am' it seems people nowadays think 'I think, therefore I am *right*'. Personal 'truth' being all important.

So much of my work (such as the illustrations in this book) uses very simple elements: circles, squares, right angle lines and 45-degree lines. It is the context and placement of these shapes that means that these simple things can be used to represent many things.

The Moon

The moon is an everyday thing. Unlike the sun,
which violently evades being directly looked at,
the moon can be viewed at length.

A flat I once lived in had big bay windows.
At certain times of the year, I could watch the moon
move from window pane to window pane like
a comic strip. I could never see it actually moving,
only when I looked away and back would I notice it
had crept across the framed piece of night sky.
This small act always reminded me that we are on
a moving planet and not as static as the solidity of
the earth makes us think.

Nonsense

One of my favourite people who used nonsense in their work is Ivor Cutler, a Scottish poet, musician and humorist. His grumpy exterior belies the playfulness of his writing and music. I was lucky enough to see him perform a couple of times; he would come on stage wearing many coats that would be removed one by one in between harmonium led songs. If the crowd cheered or clapped too loudly he would put his fingers in his ears until they stopped. Later, I found out he was a member of the Noise Abatement Society. In his songs and spoken word pieces, shoplifters literally lift shops or too small balloons fail to assuage hunger.

Can nonsense be used to challenge authority? Not the idiotic kind (although why not?) but the kind that is knowing. If we refuse to play by the rules that are put upon us and don't let on what it is we are trying to do, how can those in charge undermine it?

In a world that seems to require things to be more and more concrete, nonsense is a weapon against homogenization. They can call us ridiculous; we would already know we are!

Handwriting*

I WROTE THIS
WITH MY
HAND

---

*Will handwriting become redundant?

Woods

I grew up near some woods, which were on
a private drive leading to a theme park. The child-
me saw them as huge and the adventures I had there
seemed to attest to this. Going back, as an adult,
I realised that they are very small and not very deep.
This doesn't change how I feel about them.

Now I have some other woods near where
I live that I walk in. These are not huge either but
bigger than the ones I played in when I was young.

I'm still filled with excitement entering a wood:
the dappled light and coolness on a sunny day; the
sound of rain on leaves; the many bird calls. Entering
a wood I feel in touch with the past, people of all
times have walked through scenes like these and
woods, at their best, have changed little.

The Cinema

A lot of cinema now feels more like a theme park
ride: thrilling, predictable and safe. My favourite
times watching films at the cinema are when the plot
isn't the most important aspect of the film, so I don't
know what is going to happen and I have no way of
predicting it. Films that, if I watched at home,
I would probably fall asleep halfway through, but at
the cinema I can give my full attention.

The slowness of the films I like, the darkness
of the cinema and the lack of distractions, mean
you can get lost in them if you let yourself.
Sometimes I realise by the end of a film no one
has made a sound and my breathing has become
slow and shallow. Films by the Thai director
Apichatpong Weerasethakul have this effect on me.
He is known for his languid films and willingness
to remain on a scene for a long time. People often
find the static long shots problematic, calling
them pretentious or pointless. This comes from an
expectation of meaning and entertainment. These
shots are no different from a scene in real life that
we would never expect meaning from. We wouldn't
call a view of nature pretentious.

The film *Memoria,* from 2021 (his first non-Thai language film), gives you many instances of being able to look beyond the main focal point of a scene without the worry of missing some important plot point. The film starts with a woman hearing a bang that no one else hears. It doesn't give you much in the way of a neat ending or plot. Because of this is it totally unpredictable. You need to let go of needing to understand. This, along with the darkness, the quiet and sitting still for 90 minutes or more allows a unique experience in today's world: the gift of concentrating on a single thing for an extended period without interruption.

I usually go to the cinema in the day between 11:30 am and 2 pm when it is quietest. I like going to the cinema on my own and the cinema-goers at this time of the day are often on their own too. Watching films around midday means when I come out it is still light. This is something I have always enjoyed: the contrast between the darkness of the cinema and the slight shock that it is still light outside, as you return to the world, much the same as you left it, from the one you have visited.

Doing Nothing

There is a Taoist saying: 'do nothing and all will be done'. People tend to misunderstand it (as I might have) and get quite annoyed at the idea of doing nothing and expecting something. I don't think that's what it means, I *think* it means going with the flow and letting things happen naturally.

In a lot of my life, I am happy to be led by the nature of things and find the simplest route to answer problems. This doesn't mean a life without effort, but it does mean I don't try and enforce my will on things that resist it – the square peg and round hole analogy.

We have created a world that so often goes against how we should naturally live in it; building things that are meant to save us time, or make life easier, but end up distancing us from simple joys. Struggle in modern life is celebrated, regardless if it is necessary or not. In Brian Eno and Peter Schmidt's *Oblique Strategies* (a box of cards with creative suggestions), one of the cards says: 'Don't be afraid of things because they're easy to do.' Maybe we need to do more nothing and notice when good things are already being done.

Empty Matchboxes

I always loved matchboxes as a child. England's Glory was my favourite and, back then, it had the rough sides to strike the match on, which smelt wonderful after use.

There is something about the way you slide open the box that makes the reveal of the contents more thrilling.

I never really knew what to put in the boxes (occasionally small bones or dead insects were put in there), but it wasn't as important as having a box with the prospect of finding something it could give a home.

Years later I made a tiny beast-like figure called a Beast in a Box, which came in a matchbox. It was naively made with a surprisingly benign expression for something called a beast. The whole package was a nod to my younger self, who would have found the beast, and its box, very exciting.

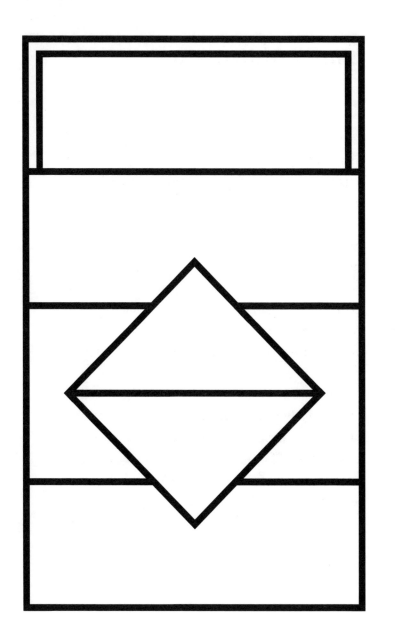

101

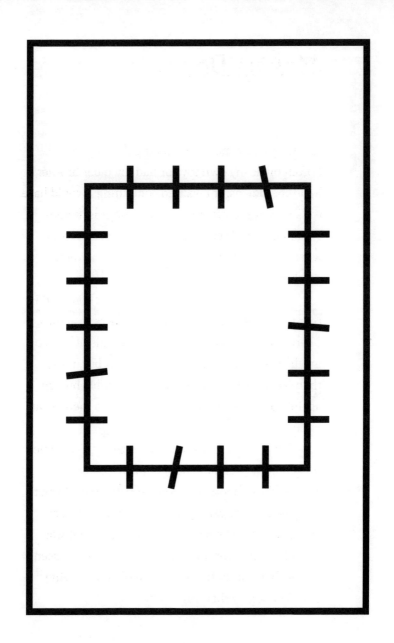

102

Making Do

I grew up in a time when making do was normal.
I often made my own toys or had my older brother's
hand-me-downs. If I wanted something I would have
to save up for it, often over many months, before
I could have it. Mending clothes was normal and
when I was a child my jeans were rarely without
patched up knees.

A clear memory of mine from my childhood is
that many cars would have coat hangers as aerials.
There was a trend of breaking the aerials off cars or
maybe they got snapped in car washes but, rather
than pay to have it replaced (and probably broken
again) someone realised you could use a metal coat
hanger in its place.

I'm not sure if this became a 'thing,' but some
people would bend the hanger into decorative
shapes, the diamond being the most simple. I can't
imagine this happening now, it would be seen as
embarrassing. Maybe it was back then and it was
just within my working class world that it was seen
as OK, but I never had any sense of people being
embarrassed by their ingenuity.

Magnets

Given more than one magnet, I can not help but play
with them. Bringing the north poles slowly closer until
their attraction suddenly snaps them together, causing
me to jump. Or introducing the south poles that repel
each other, no matter how hard I try to push the two
sides nearer. Their nature, of invisible power, brings
out a playfulness that takes the oddness of magnets
and magnetism, for granted.

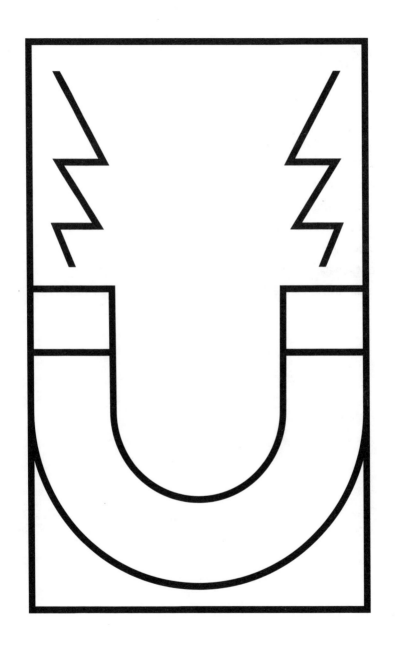

105

Getting Lost

It's harder to get lost in the modern world than it used to be. Many of us carry around a device that will give us directions to almost anywhere in the world.

In London, where I live, I often try to get lost in the city centre. When I first moved here in the '90s it was easy: the streets would often make you feel like you were heading one way, but their non-parallel nature would be taking you off in another direction altogether. Now I try to get lost but all I do is go down streets I have never been before until, quite quickly, I reach somewhere that I know.

Getting lost can be fun but also terrifying. When you realise you don't know where you are, or how to get to where you are going, a panic sets in. I guess that is why it's used in so many horror films. It is an innate human fear.

Trees

I have always liked trees: silver birch, willow and oak were some of my favourites growing up, now I can add ginkgo, Japanese red maple and giant sequoia to that list. When I was younger I tried to grow bonsai trees, or rather look after young ones bought from the local garden centre, their tiny beauty seemed to fit in with my love of fantasy and miniature things. At the time I didn't make the connection between us and trees until, much later, I saw the structure of our veins in isolation.

Our veins, which are so dense* they create an outline of a human, look just like the branches and roots of trees. When I saw this, a new connection was made with something that I already loved. We often talk of being in nature rather than being a part of it. But we are the same. Made up of the same problem-solving evolution.

---

*An adult human has approximately 60,000 miles of blood vessels in their body.

Routine

I have some small routines in my life that give
me pleasure. One of my favourites is going to the
cinema in the day, on my own, when the cinema
is a quiet, non popcorn-munching, place. The
cinemas I go to are either in Mayfair, Bloomsbury
or Soho. The films usually finish around 2 pm
and then I head over to the Coach & Horses* on
Greek Street to read a book and have a pint. The
Coach & Horses doesn't serve food or coffee (what
I have recently found out is called a wet pub), so it's
usually not as busy in the day as other pubs in the
area, although past 5 pm it is packed.

Having gone in for the past couple of years
I have become a regular, even though I visit, at most,
once a week and I live eight miles away. Ali, who
runs the Coach, started asking me what I had been
doing with my day, from that we would talk about
films and then all kinds of other things. I have
always wanted to have a pub that I could walk into
and be greeted with recognition. I now have that
with the Coach & Horses.

---

*The Coach and Horses is a very popular pub name. Confusingly there are
three just in Soho. I have overheard half of conversations that are always
the same: 'I *am* in the Coach and Horses where are you?'

This little routine is something that guarantees to make me happier (even better if the day starts with a chilly swim). Recently I have added an extra stop to my routine. After the pub, I make my way down to the river and head over to the Royal Festival Hall, Level 5, to the National Poetry Library.

The library is small but well-stocked. When looking for a poet I like I am often presented with almost everything they have published, including rare editions, which can be thrilling but also a little overwhelming. One of the last times I was there I was looking for work by Ian Hamilton Finlay (a Scottish, word-based artist) and found plain green folders in the section, alphabetically, where he should be. Inside the folders were small booklets and fold-out publications with minimal words, usually relating to the sea, each feeling like a small treasure.

Once I'm finished there, and if I have time, I will walk along the Southbank to London Bridge station, passing famous landmarks and tourists on holiday, as I make my way home.

Masking Tape

Over the years I have had a lot of conversations about tape. I have used it professionally in painting for a long time, but there are lots of people out there who also seem to take joy in masking tape.

My favourites are a pink tape, that can be used on paper without ripping it, and something called masking tape for curves.

If I post a video of me removing tape from one of my paintings someone will always ask 'how do you make circles with tape!?'

Many years ago I saw a film of the artist Michael Craig-Martin in front of a blank pink canvas; using a scalpel he peeled tape, invisible up to that point, to reveal the black lines of one of his diagrammatic images. I realised this was how I could make my geometric drawings into paintings. I googled: masking tape for curves and found: masking tape for curves, a crimped tape that allows you to follow non-liner lines. The reaction to the revelation of the tape's existence is a sense of wonder that it even exists.*

---

*Recently, I gave a children's workshop where they could use masking tape for curves to recreate my *Round* paintings. Whereas adults are amazed at a tape that curves, the children took its existence as obvious: why wouldn't it exist?

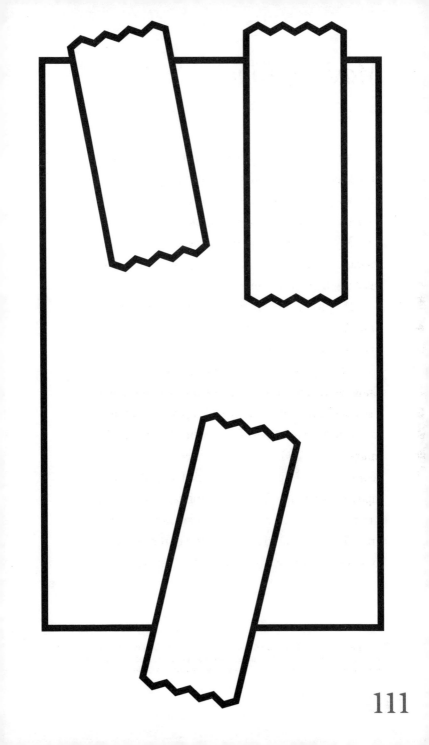

111

Negative Space

We don't tend to think too much about the space
between things, but it is often what is not there,
rather than what is, that is important. Drawing
a simple outline can suggest something of huge
density but the lines themselves, which can be very
delicate, are making sense of space; framing nothing
to create something.

Graphic designers get very excited (and
annoyed) about something called 'kerning' which
is the balance of space between letters. Mainly, it is
about aesthetics and different designers will argue
about the *right* way to kern, but sometimes bad
kerning* can lead to miscommunication, changing
how a word is read. Empty space is important.

---

*I have a song, that I sometimes sing at talks, called 'Close But Never Touching'
which is about kerning. The last time I performed it was for the Typographic
Circle, which, sadly, isn't as clandestine as the Magic Circle.

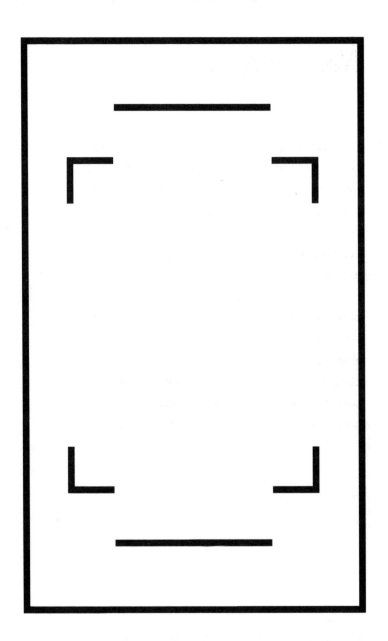

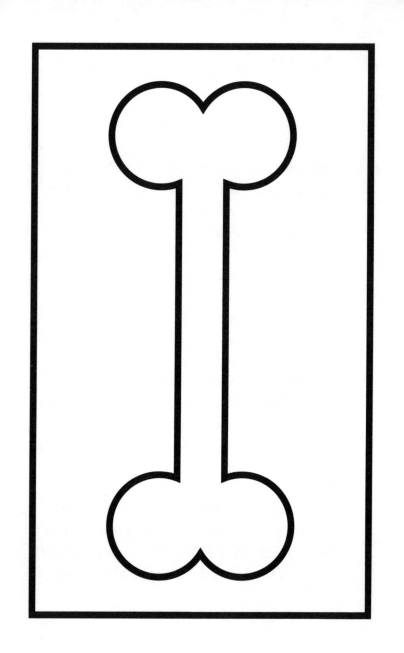

114

Skeletons

The woods where I spent a lot of my youth and early teens were a place where I came into close contact with animals. These animals, with the exception of birds, were mainly dead.

It was here I came across the only mole I have ever seen. I was surprised at how small is was and how violent its claws appeared. I hid it in the undergrowth and would come back to check on its state as the days went on.

At some point, the flesh would all be gone and just the bones would be left. I would usually only take the skull. But with the mole, I took the claws too. I didn't have lots of skulls, I don't want to make this out to be an obsession, but I always found the similarities with our own skeletons more interesting than the differences. We are not that different. We come from the same plan.

Years later I sometimes become aware of my skeleton and it makes me think back to the woods; making me aware of what is lying under my skin. If I think about it too much I find it hard to breathe.

Repetition

I'm a fan of repetition.

Not the kind that is pointless or dogged, but the kind that transforms through its repetition.

The best minimal art and music does this. Through repetition, we are able to make the most ordinary things sublime.

117

Laughing

I like laughing. Are there people who don't? There
are definitely people who seem not to laugh much
– or not around me. My pet hate is when people say
'That's so funny', but don't laugh. That is not how
funny things work, if it is funny, laugh, that's the
protocol.

There have been quite a few times in my life
when I have desperately wanted to laugh but the
situation has meant it would be inappropriate to
do so (this doesn't include when this happened at
school, which it did a lot). Usually at a quiet concert
or something serious.

One of those times was at my nan's funeral.
The vicar asked us to turn to the appropriate
page in the hymn book and sing along. The noise
that was made was so tuneless that me and my
brother started laughing. Why is it that we can't
stop laughing when we are in a situation where we
shouldn't laugh? It seems like a fault in evolution.

Choices

'The ultimate, hidden truth of the world is that it is something that we make, and could just as easily make differently.'

This quote was used by Adam Curtis in his series *Can't Get You Out of My Head.* It says everything I wanted to say but more succinctly. It is taken from the book *The Utopia of Rules: On Technology, Stupidity, and the Secret Joys of Bureaucracy* by David Graeber.

Everything

'*Every view of things that is not strange is false*'
Paul Valéry

Everything in the world is a kind of magic.
No matter how ordinary something may seem,
viewed from the perspective that we are spinning on
a globe at 1000 miles an hour in a vast universe,
it becomes something incredible and odd.

121

Notes

Lost Ordinary Magic
The title *Lost Ordinary Magic* is taken from Leonard Cohen's 1966 book *Beautiful Losers*. The part of the book it appears in is a grandiose, and funny, lament on constipation. The protagonist is suffering terribly and is begging for relief. I've never read anything like it, before or since, and there are many great lines but the sentence 'lost ordinary magic' stood out.

Ways of Hearing – Damon Krukowski (2019 MIT Press)
Damon was also the drummer for Galaxie 500 who had three albums out in the late '80s and early '90s. They have continued to be one of my favourite bands. He still makes music with his partner Naomi Yang who was also one-third of Galaxie 500.

Magnum
Magnum is a rock band from my hometown formed in 1972 but had their biggest success in the '80s. They were the first band I saw live and the lead singer was the best man at my aunt and uncle's wedding. He dressed in all white including a bolero jacket and white baseball boots with a B on one ankle and a C (his initials) on the other in an Old English script.

Not long ago, I was waiting for a rail replacement bus service in Tamworth when a small, grumbling, long-haired man walked past me wearing a leather jacket and a Magnum T-shirt. I recognised him instantly. It was Bob.

The Barnyard Epithet and Other Obscenities; Notes on the Chicago Conspiracy Trial – J. Anthony Lukas (1970 Perennial Library)

I bought this book partly because I recognised some of the counterculture characters that appeared in the trial such as Abbie Hoffman (author of *Steal This Book*) and the poet Allen Ginsberg. The story of the trial from the book was made into a film in 2020 called *The Trial of the Chicago 7*.

Sarah Records (1987 – 1995)

Most of my favourite bands on Sarah were called the something: The Field Mice, The Sea Urchins and The Orchids. 'The Something' was all the rage in the indie pop world – probably because of The Smiths.

The Sea Urchins wrote songs at age seventeen that sounded like they had been around much longer. Lyrics like: 'The end can't be the same for everyone'

Notes

taken from a song called *Cling Film* which was on their first release: a cheaply produced flexi disc, have stuck with me over the years.

The Field Mice sang sad songs about breaking up and sometimes confused sexuality. One of my favourites, called *So Said Kay*, ends with the lyrics: 'She reached in and placed a string of lights around this heart of mine'. Much later I found out all the lyrics in this song were taken from *Desert Hearts,* a 1985 film by Donna Deitch. The story is centred around a 1950s love affair between a woman staying in a guest house in Nevada to get a divorce, and a local, younger woman. I've now seen it and it is a great film of its time. The imagery I had in my mind however, which was wintry, is totally opposite from the dusty heat of the film.

Clouds
For a short time, I worked in an office shared with the *Idler* magazine. I was designing a magazine called *Good For Nothing*; we had a small part of the office which was in Hatton Gardens. The Idlers were hardly ever there, coming in when the magazine needed to go to print in a mess of paper and ruffled hair. Even though

they championed idleness they all had side projects. The designer of the magazine, Gavin Pretor-Pinney, founded the Cloud Appreciation Society in 2005 which now has over 60,000 members from all over the world.

Against Creativity – Oli Mould (2018 Verso)
I was interested in this book because I have a mural in Covent Garden that says 'Creativity is in All of Us' and I wanted to see what someone might say against this. The book is mainly an attack on the capitalist use of creativity (rather than creativity itself) including something like my mural – which happens to be on the side of an art store.

Memoria – Apichatpong Weerasethakul (2021)
The original release of the film went on tour in America playing in only one cinema on any given date. The audience watching it would be the only one in the world watching the film at that point (in the same way a live band can only seen by one group of people at a time). Originally the film was only ever going to be shown in cinemas but you can now buy it on DVD.

Notes

Ivor Cutler (1923 – 2006)

When I first moved to London in 1996, I would visit
Charing Cross Road which, at the time, was still full of
bookshops. Blackwell's had a section of underground
literature that introduced me to a whole new world of
writing but they also stocked books by Ivor Cutler in the
poetry section. The books were tiny and, often, signed in
a biro scrawl. They were filled with nonsensical stories
that I didn't always understand but I found inspirational.
These books are still some of the most treasured items
that I own and still a constant source of inspiration.

Taoism

I first heard about Taoism (in a philosophical sense)
when reading about it in the *Idler* magazine (before I
shared an office with them), who were obviously drawn
to the perceived central idea of doing nothing.

Choses Tues – Paul Valéry (1930)

I found 'Every view of things that is not strange is false'
in a list of quotes written on walls during the 1968 French
student uprising. Looking into where it was taken from,
it seems to be a book from 1930 which has never been

translated into English. The title is translated by Google as *Things Killed*, which I think might be a bad translation and ruins the rhyme, but I like it. The book also contains the quote: 'Small unexplained facts always contain enough to upset all explanations of big facts.'

Wolpe Pegasus

The typeface used throughout this book is Wolpe Pegasus designed by Berthold Wolpe in 1937 and digitised by Toshi Omagari for Monotype in 2017. I was lucky enough to visit the Monotype archives before the typeface was made commercially available; opening grey archive boxes stuffed with typographic treasures, I was excited by all the new characters I saw.

Berthold Wolpe is one of my heroes. His book cover designs for Faber, which often used purely hand-lettered typography, have been an influence on my own work. He also designed the more well-known typeface Albertus which can be seen in use on many street signs all over London, although, sadly, not the street I live on.

Errata

'...nothing breaks a proofreader's heart like a mistake you find after the book comes out.'
Mieko Kawakami – *All the Lovers in the Night*

There is something about missing errors in writing that is linked to our ability to be fooled by magic. Spelling mistakes are often easier to spot but it is the the erroneous words that are tricky (I put in the extra 'the' on purpose). Our brain removes words that are not needed or fills in the blanks. The world we experience is an edited one.

Why, the moment you have something printed, mistakes reveal themselves seems to be a cruel magic. They were there all along but, after reading and reading, they sit there unseen, hiding in plain sight. Once seen, however, they become stark and obvious, like a revealed trick.

In Mieko Kawakami's book *All the Lovers in the Night* the protagonist is a proofreader. She is devastated to see a mistake in a book she proofread. A fellow proofreader consoles her saying 'there's no such thing as a perfect book', but it is of little comfort.

I wonder what it is like to be a proofreader, in a world full of mistakes.